WATCH/GUARD DOGS

BY MATTHEW NEWMAN

EDITED BY DR. HOWARD SCHROEDER
Professor in Reading and Language Arts
Dept. of Elementary Education
Mankato State University

**PRODUCED & DESIGNED BY
BAKER STREET PRODUCTIONS**

CRESTWOOD HOUSE

LIBRARY OF CONGRESS CATALOGING IN PUBLICATION DATA

Newman, Matthew.
  Watch/guard dog.

  (Working dogs)
  SUMMARY: Discusses the history, training, uses, and breeds of guard dogs, including personal-protection dogs and industrial security dogs.
  1. Watchdogs--Juvenile literature. (1. Watchdogs) I. Schroeder, Howard. II. Title. III. Series
SF428.8.N49   1985   636.7'0886   85-19542
ISBN 0-89686-287-9 (lib. bdg.)

International Standard Book Number:	**Library of Congress Catalog Card Number:**
Library Binding 0-89686-287-9	85-19542

ILLUSTRATION CREDITS

All photography by
  Alan Leder

CRESTWOOD HOUSE
Hwy. 66 South, Box 3427
Mankato, MN 56002-3427

Table of contents

1.
Max: a personal-protection dog

Max is a three-year-old German shepherd that lives with the Travers' family in New York City. Mr. and Mrs. Travers, along with their two daughters, Kelly and Jess, all helped raise Max. They got him when he was still a puppy.

Max is a personal-protection dog.

Like everyone else in the house, Max has certain duties. His most important duty is to protect his owners. When the family goes away on vacation, Max watches over the property. When a family member has to go out at night alone, Max goes along. And when Mr. and Mrs. Travers go out with friends, Max stays home with the children.

Sometimes, Kelly and Jess take Max for walks. At a busy intersection, he always sits patiently by their side. He waits for their signal to move. He seems totally relaxed and almost lazy.

However, all of Max's senses are alive and alert. He hears the traffic and watches people moving in many directions. His nose picks up scents from as far away as five hundred yards. He takes in new sights, scents, and sounds every moment.

"Heel, Max." Kelly says.

Max obeys immediately and moves to Kelly's left side. Kelly never has to repeat a command, or stomp her foot. As they cross the street, Max watches the traffic to make sure it is safe.

Most dogs are naturally protective of their owners. But Max is a very special kind of guard dog. He is a professional, personal-protection dog.

Mr. and Mrs. Travers both have jobs and are very wealthy. They travel a lot, and feel they need extra protection for their home and family. They do not want a gun in the house. That is why they selected a professional, personal-protection dog.

When they made their decision to find a dog, they went to see Mike Haggerty. Mr. Haggerty runs the Haggerty School for Canine Arts in New York. They told Mr. Haggerty they needed a special guard dog. The dog would have to be gentle around children. He would have to like men and women. The dog could not be too shy, or too mean, and he would have to obey at all times.

Mike thought about the Travers' protection needs. Then, using his own expert judgement, he chose Max. Max was only three months old at the time. Still, Mike felt that Max would be the perfect match for the Travers family. He knew this because of Max's breeding, or family history. The male and female dog who produced Max came from a long line of good guard dogs.

Besides, Max was already showing many of the signs of a top guard dog. He was very alert, he was curious, and eager to please. And, he was frisky in a good-natured way.

Like any professional, however, Max would have to go to school to really learn his craft. Max and Mr. Travers attended classes together for eighteen months.

They started with "K-9 Kindergarten" training. Here, Max learned basic obedience. This meant learning basic commands, such as "sit," and "heel." Next, Max trained on an obstacle course. He learned how to scale twenty-foot high walls. Max also

Max is being trained on an obstacle course.

learned how to go through tunnels and windows.

The final stage of training was called man-work. Max had to learn how to seize a weapon and how to attack on command. Mr. Travers was taught to use special commands, spoken in a foreign language, so that only he would have the power to turn Max on a criminal. At each level of training, Max was tested. He had to test perfectly at every level before he graduated.

Before he began training, Max was a good dog. He was gentle, loyal, and friendly. After training, he was

In the final stage of training, Max was taught to attack on command. The trainer wears padded clothing.

still a good dog. He still liked his family and enjoyed being with Kelly and Jess. He looked about the same as before. The only real difference was that his natural abilities had been sharpened. Instead of being a good guard dog, he was now a professional guard dog.

Max was such a good guard dog that he was asked to act in a motion picture. In real life, Max was always a "good guy." In the movie, the director wanted him to play a "bad guy." The movie was called *Shamus,* and starred Burt Reynolds. Reynolds played a New York detective named Mike Shamus. Max played a vicious attack dog.

Mike Haggerty served as Max's trainer on the set. At one time, Mr. Haggerty was chief of the United States Army's "K-9 Corps." He had worked with many good guard dogs over the years. Max was one of his favorites.

In one scene, Max was supposed to attack Burt Reynolds, who was sitting in a car. They waited for the director's cue. Finally, everyone was quiet on the set.

"Action," the director said.

"Get em," Mike whispered.

Suddenly, Max crouched and snarled. As ordered, he charged the car window. Behind the glass, Reynolds froze, pretending to be scared. Afterwards, Max trotted back to his trainer's side. The crew applauded his acting. Max had played the bad guy very well.

2.

Watch/guard dogs in history

Why have dogs earned the title of man's best friend? Could it be because of their long service as guardians? For as long as they have been our friends, they have also been our protectors.

Sulukis are one of the oldest breeds, or types of dog, to serve in the home. These dogs were used as guard dogs ten thousand years ago by Egyptian kings. Sulukis guarded the kings' houses.

The Egyptians also used greyhounds and mastiffs. These breeds were valued as hunters and pets, as well as guard dogs. Egyptian families cared a great deal for their dogs. When a favorite dog died, the family set aside a special time for grief.

The sheepdog is one of the earliest forms of the watch dog. For hundreds of years many breeds have served as herders of sheep, goats, and cattle. Briards, Bouviers, and collies are all types of sheepdog.

Sheepdogs have amazing talents. They can sense when one sheep out of a flock of two hundred sheep has wandered off. To keep sheep in line, they can nip the heels of the sheep without drawing blood.

Sheepdogs make good protection dogs.

Before guns, and before battles were fought on horseback, many breeds were used by armies. The Romans used Rottweilers as sentries, or lookout guards. They protected the soldiers' food from thieves.

During the Middle Ages, from A.D. 476 to A.D. 1453, the average man's dog was expected to earn his keep. There was no police force and crime was widespread. Dogs were needed to serve as guards for children and homes. The art of training guard dogs had not been perfected. Still, owners took this job seriously. Dogs were trained to obey spoken commands. They also followed commands given by playing notes on a horn.

The Romans used Rottweilers as guard dogs.

12

By the 1880's, people were arguing over which breeds — small or large — were better guards. In 1911, a New York Times newspaper story told about eighteen dogs being sent to Hong Kong, China. Their task was to protect the property of European businessmen. And by the 1930's, German shepherds were being used as guards at industrial sites and museums.

It was during the 1940's that formal obedience training was started by Willy Necker. Mr. Necker helped to develop the American Kennel Club's obedience trials. In these trials (tests), dogs were rated on how well they acted around people. To win a Companion Title, a dog had to behave for his or her owner. To win a Utility Title, the dog had to show direction and tracking skills. Other titles were given for different kinds of obedience.

Mr. Necker began many obedience trial clubs around America. For the first time, people began to see obedience training as an important part of being a dog owner.

Today, the watch/guard dog industry is booming. Trained dogs are worth thousands of dollars. Over four thousand such dogs "work" in New York alone. Guard dogs are also used by the Federal Bureau of Investigation, armed forces, and local police. These dogs even patrol the White House!

In this book, we'll focus on watch and guard dogs that protect people and businesses.

3.

Who needs a professional?

We all value protection. This is especially true for the senior citizen, or for the woman who lives alone. It is also true for the junkyard trader and the farmer. Many of us need special protection. Watch and guard dogs can help fill this need.

Does this mean that most people need a professional guard dog? The answer is no. The same is true for most businesses. The cost, training, and management of these dogs is beyond the ability of most people. Besides, there are other ways to gain protection.

In fact, very few people need a professional guard dog. For most of us, a good watchdog is all we might need.

People who try to turn their dogs into semi-professional guards are making a big mistake. There is no such thing as a "semi-professional" guard dog. Such animals can become dangerous long before they are useful. Training a professional guard dog is a job that should be done by an expert.

Selecting a dog for it's natural guard talents is different. This is something that the average person can do. There are about one hundred and thirty different breeds from which to choose.

There are many choices

Among large and small breeds, there are a variety of guard dog types. They range from the tiny barker, the Chihuahua, to the huge and kindly Irish wolfhound. Each breed offers a special blend of physical skills and has a special temperament. A dog may be small and even-tempered. It might be small and nervous. It might be large and shy or it could also be large and outgoing. No matter what size or temper-

Watchdogs come in all sizes and colors.

Small watchdogs are called alarm dogs.

ament, nearly all breeds are protective to some degree.

There are alarm dogs who simply bark, and alarm dogs who bark and have a bite to back it up. There are breeds which pose a physical threat because of their size. And there are "man-stoppers." Choosing the right breed of dog will probably be your most important decision as an owner.

Choosing the right individual dog is your next most important decision. You have the choice of a male or a female. Dogs of both sexes are protective. Usually, a male dog is bolder, and has greater size and strength.

The value of a purebred

You can choose either a crossbreed or a purebred. A crossbreed is a dog produced by two or more different types of dog. A purebred is one produced by two dogs of the same breed.

Experts urge owners to choose a purebred. A purebred is likely to be registered with the American Kennel Club. Its registration tells its breeding history, or pedigree. You can trace a dog's family tree over the past fifty years. If relatives had good guard talents, your dog may follow this pattern.

Certain breeds have deeply-rooted protection skills. This is because of inbreeding. Inbreeding is when dogs of the same breed are mated together over many years. For these dogs, abilities show regardless of training. This is the reason German shepherds, Doberman pinschers, and Rottweilers are rated as the top guard dog types. Bull-mastiffs, Weimaraners, and Airedale terriers are also highly ranked.

Remember that any dog, regardless of breed, has an individual personality. So, choosing the right breed doesn't guarantee a good guard dog. For example, you might find an overly shy German shepherd. Or, you could find a tiny alarm dog who acts like a determined man-stopper. The owner has to be careful when selecting a guard dog.

Rottweilers are big enough to be "man-stoppers."

4.

Large guard dogs

There are two guard dog types among large breeds. First, there is the man-stopper. These dogs can more than meet a criminal head on. Second, there are dogs which pose a physical threat. These dogs may be overpowered by a person, but not easily. In most cases, females are smaller than males.

German shepherds have long served as herding and farm dogs. In modern times, their roles as police, guide, and watchdogs is well-known. By far, more guard dogs come from this breed than any other.

In temperament, few compare with the shepherd. They are gentle, loyal, and brave. They do not get overly excited in the face of danger. Shepherds have a blend of speed and strength. They are large enough to be man-stoppers. They are swift enough to pursue. Male shepherds stand at about twenty-five inches (64 cm) tall at the shoulder. They weigh about eighty-five pounds (38.6 kg).

Doberman pinschers were developed by Ludwig Dobermann of Germany in the early 1900's. Dobermans have an ideal body build. This dog does not just look like it means business. It can back it up!

Dobermans have six hundred and fifty pounds of pressure per square inch (45 kg per square centimeter) when they bite.

Dobermans have a reputation for being "one-man" dogs. Still, they can make fine house pets. Obedience training, however, is strongly urged. Male Dobermans stand twenty-seven inches (69 cm) tall at the shoulder. They weigh about eighty pounds (36.4 kg).

Rottweilers are one of the finest guard-dog breeds. They have a long history as guards. During the days of the Roman Empire, they herded livestock. At night, they often guarded supply dumps. Rottweilers do not look very fierce. But looks do not tell the whole story. Stocky and muscular, they are powerful man-stoppers.

The bull-mastiff is a combination of the bulldog and the mastiff. He is a popular choice for those who live in the city because he is quiet. He also is eager to please. Male bull-mastiffs stand twenty-seven inches (69 cm) tall and weigh about one hundred and fifteen pounds (52 kg).

Medium and small guard dogs

Among medium and small breeds, there are fewer man-stoppers. Some of these breeds might be overmatched by a criminal. So, their main function is to warn or scare, rather than to defend. Still, small size does have its advantages. Small dogs may be well suited to a smaller home, and they make good driving companions. Besides, some make fierce defenders in spite of their size!

Like all terriers, Airedales have very good guarding abilities. Named after a valley in England, they have a history of police work.

Sheepdogs are very protective.

Belgian sheepdogs are very protective. Some have been known to gently try herding their owners! Males reach twenty-five inches (64 cm) in height and weigh fifty-five to sixty-five pounds (25-29.5 kg).

Boxers were originally developed in Germany. They offer a lot as guards in looks alone. They have short, brown coats and square muzzles. Boxers are famous for their gentle manner around children. Males reach twenty-four inches (61.5 cm) in height and weigh about seventy pounds (31.8 kg).

Kerry blue-terriers come from Ireland. They are known for being loyal and playful. They are small, but very brave. These terriers have thick, bluish-grey coats. Males weigh about thirty-five to forty pounds (16-18 kg).

These young people are practicing hand signals with their sheepdog.

5.

Using natural skills

You have decided you do not need a professional guard dog. Still, you want to make the best of your dog's natural skills as a watchdog. What do you do?

The first four to six months in any dog's life is the "puppy period." A pup needs this time to grow and develop. During this time the pup learns to become comfortable with its home and family.

By seven months of age, your dog has already learned many things. It is housebroken and knows you are its owner. The dog knows where it lives, and who feeds it. The dog may have naturally begun to bark at strangers. It knows what "no" means. In other words, the dog is already showing signs of being a good watchdog.

At the same time, your dog may also have learned some bad habits. Maybe it barks at the telephone, growls at your friends, or likes to chase strangers. The dog may even have tried to bite someone who did not deserve it. It thinks it is being a good watchdog. However, the dog has not really learned how to use his skills.

Training a dog for your needs is very important.

Obedience training

It is time to start obedience training. For the everyday watchdog, this should be all the schooling your dog ever needs. Obedience lessons can begin when the dog is four to six months of age. You have the choice of doing the training at home, or taking your dog to an obedience school. Either method will work.

During obedience training, you and your dog learn together. You learn how to give the basic commands like "heel," "sit," "stay," "lie down," and "come." You learn how to give hand signals. You also learn when to give praise and when to correct the dog's mistakes. Your dog learns that it must obey, even when there are distractions present, such as other animals.

It is important to approach training with a good attitude. This means being serious about your work. If you are not serious, your dog probably will not be either.

Put aside a special time each day for the session if you're doing the training yourself. Stick to it! Lessons should only last about ten or fifteen minutes. Try to hold more than one session a day. Your dog will learn more quickly.

Avoid feeding the dog or letting the dog be too active before a session. The dog needs to be relaxed.

As you train your dog, take it through each lesson step-by-step. Never rush the dog. Repeat each lesson until he or she masters it.

Gradually, you can introduce new skills. At some point, your dog will begin to be able to handle two commands at once. For example, it may learn to "sit-stay." This means he should stay in the sit position until you say to move. Try not to confuse the dog by teaching him too much too soon.

Don't expect miracles

Certain dogs train more easily than others. Others might learn slowly. Some dogs perform perfectly —until another animal is around. Other dogs are not bothered by other animals. Some dogs remember what they learn, while others seem to easily forget their lessons. As you work with your dog, you will learn how much praise is needed. You will also learn how to correct your dog to keep him on the right track.

Do not expect a dog to learn something his breeding has not prepared him for. For example, a poodle will never learn to be a man-stopper. Some breeds are just naturally good guards. Some dogs can be taught to be good guards. Other dogs will never be good guards. Remember, selecting the right breed

A good watchdog has to learn to be obedient.

and the right individual dog can make a big difference.

Regardless of a dog's natural guard abilities, obedience work always makes for a better pet. Special problems, such as digging, chewing, and chasing, can be cured with the help of obedience training.

6.

Who needs one?

What kind of person needs a professional personal-protection dog? The person might be an executive who lives alone in a high-rise apartment, or a wealthy person with jewelry and securities to protect. It might be an ex-spy or a person living on a yacht. It might be an antique car collector. Many types of people feel a need for these dogs.

The personal-protection dog is said to be "attack-trained." This means it only attacks on command from its owner. In this way, the personal-protection dog is different from the plant security dog.

The personal-protection dog performs its job at many locations. Not all of these areas are enclosed. No matter where it is, this dog is on the job. Whether in the yard, street, or the car, it is expected to act as a guard. At any moment, its man-stopping abilities may be called upon.

Controlling the dog

At the same time, the personal-protection dog must know when to relax. For example, this dog

A guard dog must know when to relax.

often works around children and neighbors. It must know better than to charge the person who delivers the mail. If a guest arrives, the dog must stop growling upon its owner's command. If a stranger comes near, the dog must alert in a calm way. If someone waves, the dog cannot read this as an attack.

In short, the personal-protection dog has a firm hold on the use of force. It is under the complete control of its owner. The dog resists distractions and accepts the presence of other animals. False alarms do not bother these dogs.

Being under control does not mean having a false sense of security. Even if the dog is not using his skills most of the time, the dog knows there may be a time when it must do so.

Taking on a personal-protection dog requires a big commitment. The dog may cost thousands of dollars. Both the dog and the owner must go through months of training. If the dog abuses its power, the owner will be held responsible.

Professional trainers and breeders will not give an attack-trained dog to just anybody. Customers must fill out an application form. The trainer/breeder studies the applicant's needs. It is he or she, not the owner, who selects the type of dog to meet the customer's needs.

An attack exercise

A young woman and her dog are walking down a busy city street. At first glance, it looks as if they are simply out for a stroll.

Around the corner, two men are hiding behind a parked car. One is a professional dog trainer. The other man is an "aggression-trainer." The woman knows they are there. The dog does not. They are setting a booby-trap.

As the woman and her dog come around the corner, they see nothing wrong. They pass the first car. Nothing happens. Then they pass the second car. Suddenly, the aggression-trainer leaps out, waving a burlap sack. He moves to strike the owner. The dog reacts by seizing the attacker's arm. The arm is padded, so it does not hurt.

"Out!" the woman commands. This command stops the dog's attack. They continue walking. Soon, they are walking down the same street again. This time, the aggression-trainer jumps out from behind the first car. From then on, the dog knows that threats can come at any time.

This kind of attack exercise is really one of the final stages of personal-protection training. Before this point, there are many other skills which must first be mastered.

Special requirements

Before a dog is even accepted for training, it must meet special requirements. The dog must be over twenty-three inches (59 cm) tall, and weigh eighty or more pounds (36.4 kg). It must be thoroughly examined by a veterinarian (animal doctor).

Dogs are also screened based on intelligence and temperament. They must be bright, energetic, and eager to perform. Even if a dog shows signs of being a good guard dog student, it may not be. Only one in ten dogs is accepted for training.

First, the dog completes obedience work. Then, personal-protection training begins. Some dogs are asked to learn one hundred or more commands. In all, training can take two or three years.

The training team

The owner, a professional handler, and an aggression-trainer all work together with the dog. The owner is involved so that the dog knows who it is supposed to protect. The handler oversees the whole training process.

The aggression-trainer is very important. He or she must be as highly trained as the dog. This person serves to tease the dog in a certain way. Trainers

Aggression-trainers must be brave.

33

must have years of experience, and must be brave. They must also know how to tease in a way that teaches. This is done in a step-by-step way.

The aggression-trainer wears a padded suit during the first stages of attack-training.

Man-work, or attack-training, is carried out in many stages. Early on, the goal is to build the dog's confidence. As the dog is teased more and more, it learns how and when to defend its owner. The dog is never abused.

There is a series of repeated lessons. Each lesson builds on skills already learned. Gradually, the dog learns to use its eyes, ears, and nose to detect attackers. It learns that attacks can come from any angle.

Later, the dogs have to sharpen their skills. They must obey their owners, even amongst distractions. A gate may be left open, or another animal may be nearby. The dog must choose to obey, even when it has a chance not to do so.

As part of their training, these dogs learn to go for the gun-hand. They also learn to stop an attack on command. Being able to turn a dog off is just as important as being able to turn him on.

Dogs learn to go for the gun-hand.

7.

A lonely job

Three men broke into a potato chip factory. They did not know a trained guard dog was waiting for them. The dog held the men captive for many hours. Finally, the men called to a passer-by. They wanted the police to save them!

In another case, thieves hid themselves in a department store. They hoped to sneak out the next morning. But before the store opened, they were caught. The store's guard dog sniffed them out.

The plant-security dog is different from the personal-protection dog. The security dog is usually posted in an enclosed area. It often works alone and has to make quick decisions. There is no time to hesitate. No one is there to give a command. The dog, alone, must decide if and when to attack.

Plant-security dogs often work in remote areas that are not well-lit. If trouble arises, it may be many minutes before help arrives. Some plant dogs are taught to scare off criminals by snarling and barking. Part of their job is to look as mean as possible. Other dogs are taught to stay calm and alert. They wait until a criminal is on the property and cut off their retreat.

Security dogs sometimes work with human guards.

Many stores and businesses are protected by security dogs.

Many plant dogs are custom-trained. Some dogs are taught to work in teams. If one dog is hurt, the other sounds the alarm. Dogs have also been trained to turn on lights or horns.

Why hire a dog?

Why would a dog be used instead of a human guard? Cost is one factor. Ability is another. A dog can be more alert over a longer period of time than a human. Even in the dark, a dog can see better than we can. Their hearing is seven times better than ours. Their amazing noses are a million times better than ours. A good guard dog can often do the work of two or three people.

Plant dogs need a quiet place to rest, away from people.

When they are searching out a criminal, plant dogs use their speed and tracking skills. They are able to cover whole plants in minutes. If they have to chase, they can run up to thirty-five miles an hour. And plant dogs are not gun-shy. They are taught to go for the gun-hand.

A trained plant dog will stop attacking upon command from its owner, or when the criminal ceases to struggle. Sometimes, a guard uses a whistle to signal to a dog that is many yards ahead. When the dog hears the whistle, it simply holds the prisoners captive.

When they are off-duty, plant dogs need a quiet, private place to rest. They are very much "one-man" dogs. Since their job is to watch out for strangers,

Plant dogs are a "one-man dog."

they cannot be too social. Still, they enjoy the trust
and companionship of their owners.

Training to fit the job

Business owners have different security needs. The small tavern owner might need one kind of guard dog. The construction site operator may need another type. There are different plant-security dogs from which to choose. These dogs are trained in special ways to meet different business needs.

Like all professional guard dogs, plant dogs first go through obedience training. This is followed by man-work. The final stage is on-site training.

A trainer/handler, an aggression-trainer, and the owner are all involved in the training. At first, dogs are trained on a chain. The chain allows dogs to react within a limited area. Later on, the dog learns to react off the chain.

Search skills are vital for the plant dog. It needs to be able to sniff out strange odors and hear unusual sounds. Even if a criminal cannot be seen, the dog must sense his or her presence. The criminal might be hidden in a chimney or hanging from a window-sill. Sensing the criminal quickly is the key to making a capture.

Plant dogs must also be taught to avoid poisoned meat. They are trained never to eat anything that is not given to them by their owners.

8.
Protecting the rights of watch/guard dogs

We have learned about the many useful services watch/guard dogs provide. In the home or the business, dogs have proven willing and able protectors. Few animals have served us so well. As great as this service is, we must not think of dogs simply as workers. Just like people, dogs deserve a full, happy life. They have rights, too.

An owner has the responsibility of protecting his or her dog's rights.

Some states have laws which tell what an owner's duties are. These laws state that a dog must be given good, wholesome food. It must be provided with housing that is protected from the weather. Medical care should be given when necessary. In general, a dog must be treated in a decent way.

In addition, the laws state that a dog should not be overworked, or hurt in any way. Failure to uphold these laws can result in a fine or a jail sentence.

Most of us do not need laws to tell us how to treat guard dogs. We need only look at the way they treat us. They are brave, loyal, and dependable. They are

Dogs are many things to us, but most of all, they are our friends.

more than our protectors. They are more than our pets. They are our friends.

46

Glossary

AGGRESSION-TRAINER — *A professional dog handler who teaches by teasing.*

ALARM DOG — *Any small breed of dog whose main purpose is to warn, rather than to defend.*

ATTACK-TRAINED — *A dog which is trained to attack only on command from his or her owner.*

BREED — *A special type of dog.*

COMMAND — *An order from an owner, such as "sit."*

CROSSBREED — *Offspring produced by a male and a female dog that are different breeds.*

DISTRACTION TRAINING — *Exercises which teach dogs to obey even when their attention is taken away.*

HANDLER — *The person who cares for and trains a dog.*

KENNEL — *The housing where one or more dogs live.*

MAN-WORK — *Training which involves a handler, the owner, and an aggression-trainer.*

MAN-STOPPER — *Usually a large breed of dog; one which is able to physically stop a criminal.*

OBEDIENCE-TRAINING — *Basic teaching, in which dogs learn to obey their masters on or off a leash.*

PEDIGREE — *The breeding history of a dog.*

PERSONAL-PROTECTION DOG — *An attack-trained dog that serves in the home, or anywhere his owners are.*

PLANT-SECURITY DOG — *A professionally trained dog that works in commercial-industrial areas.*

PUREBRED — *A dog produced by a male and female dog that are the same breed.*

SENTRY DOG — *A dog whose main purpose is to serve as a lookout guard.*

VETERINARIAN — *A doctor who provides medical care to animals.*

WORKING DOGS

READ ABOUT THE MANY KINDS OF DOGS THAT WORK FOR A LIVING:

HEARING-EAR DOGS

GUIDE DOGS

WATCH/GUARD DOGS

LAW ENFORCEMENT DOGS

SEARCH & RESCUE DOGS

STUNT DOGS

SLED DOGS

MILITARY DOGS

CRESTWOOD HOUSE